the LieOGRAPHY
of

BABE RUTH

The Absolutely Untrue, Totally Made Up, 100% Fake Life Story of Baseball's Greatest Slugger

by Alan Katz
illustrations by TRACY HILL

Tanglewood • Indianapolis

Published by Tanglewood Publishing, Inc.
Text © 2020 Alan Katz
Illustrations © 2020 Tracy Hill

Cover and Interior art by Tracy Hill
Design by Amy Alick Perich

Tanglewood Publishing, Inc.
1060 N. Capitol Ave., Ste. E-395
Indianapolis, IN 46204
www.tanglewoodbooks.com

Printed in the USA by Gasch Printing, LLC.
10 9 8 7 6 5 4 3 2

ISBN 978-1-939100-46-7

Library of Congress Control Number: 2020939019

Dedication:
To the New York Mets

One

Tie score. Ninth inning. Second and third, two outs. Mike Dribbleman at bat with a three-two count.

Ball four! Dribbleman jogged to first to load the bases! And everyone knew the big, big, big slugger was on deck.

The men in the crowd yelled, "Oooh!" The women in the crowd yelled, "Aaah!" And people listening at home on their radios heard all the excitement and yelled, "Wowwww!"

The seven-year-old big, big, big slugger was stepping toward the plate.

When you're a seven-year-old big, big, big slugger, and everyone in Philadelphia is

standing around the field cheering, that's a pretty special moment (especially when the game is in Baltimore, 'cause that's a long way for the entire town of Philadelphia to have traveled).

That'd be a heap of pressure for most ballplayers. But nothing, absolutely nothing bothered Ruth Herman George. Why, he had pressure for lunch every day, along with forty-two meatballs and a canned ham. Including the can.

Ruth stepped up to the plate and boldly pointed to the hot dog stand beyond the fence in center field. As he studied the stand, he said to himself, "After the game, I'm going to enjoy their all-you-can-eat hot dog special."

Now, the stand *didn't have* an all-you-can-eat hot dog special, but again, that didn't bother Ruth Herman George. Nothing did.

Ruth picked up the bat and rubbed it under his left armpit for good luck. The men in the crowd yelled, "Oooh!" The women in the crowd yelled, "Aaah!" And the people listening at home on their radios heard all the excitement and said, "What? What did he do? We can't see it! Waaaaaa!"

The pitcher looked in for the sign. Fastball. Strike one! And just like that, another fastball. Two strikes! Ruth dug into the batter's box, and as the third pitch came sailing in, he swung and sent a foul ball back into the crowd with such force that it knocked a little girl's iPhone out of her hands!

"Sorry," Ruth yelled. 'Cause although nothing bothered him, he did feel bad smashing people's things, especially when they were valuable items that wouldn't be invented until nearly a century later.

But even worse than breaking the iPhone was the fact that Ruth's mighty swing had destroyed the team's only bat. It was the bat he'd used to hit ninety-six home runs that season—in exactly that many at bats—and now it was, well, toothpicks.

"No bat, game's over!" yelled the pitcher.

"Yeah, no bat, game's over!" yelled the catcher, who often repeated what the pitcher said.

But Ruth just shrugged, got in the batter's box, and started waving an *invisible* bat. "Just throw the ball!" he barked at the pitcher.

The pitcher laughed. The catcher laughed. And Ruth Herman George just grunted.

The pitcher looked in for the sign. The catcher showed two fingers, which either meant the curveball...or two fastballs. Since the pitcher only had one ball in his glove, he decided it must have meant curveball.

He gripped the ball, glared at the batter, and released a giant curveball toward the bat-less batter.

As the pitch crossed the plate, Ruth swung—with his stiffened arm—and connected! A mighty blast! Going, going, gone!

The men in the crowd yelled, "Oooh!" The women in the crowd yelled, "Aaah!" A little kid in the crowd yelled, "He hit a grand slam with his arm? I don't believe it!" And the people at home said, "Thank you, kid! *Finally* we know what's going on!"

Ruth Herman George was a hero that day, just as he'd been all season. And just as he'd be for many seasons to come.

But his life hadn't always been so glory-filled...

Two

"It's a boy!" announced the nurse.

"It's a *big* boy!" announced the other nurse.

"Hoo boy, what a boy!" announced the doctor. "Why, he's practically a man!"

Yes, the baby was so huge at birth, it's surprising he didn't go on to play for the Giants. In fact, it's somewhat surprising he didn't play for the Giants the day he was born.

The nurses wrapped the kid in his first diaper—well actually, a queen-size blanket—and together tried to lift the kid.

"Ruth, time to give the mother her man," said the doctor. "Lou, you help."

"Yes, Dr. George," said the nurses.

"Wait! I love that name!" the kid's mother shouted. "We'll call him Ruth. Ruth Her Man. Ruth Her Man George."

The room was silent. Nurse Ruth wept. Dr. George teared up a little. And Lou bawled.

"Heyyyy, why aren't you naming him after me too?" Lou demanded to know as he whimpered.

"Frankly, your pants are a little crumpled, and you remind me of my cousin, Henry, who once stepped on my prized rose bush and caused me to lose the neighborhood flower contest and the million-dollar grand prize, and even though he said he was sorry, I never really forgave him or his clumsiness."

"I understand perfectly," said Lou as he dried his tears. "And I don't blame you one bit."

It was a nice moment in room 714 at UNCLE AN HOSPITAL.

Ruth Herman George and his mother were squooshed into the bed, and his dad passed out celebration tuna sandwiches to the doctor, the nurses, and the guy mopping

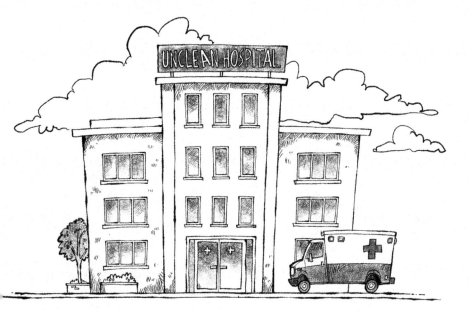

the floor in the corner. Then he gave one to his wife. But before she could take a bite, their newborn snatched it and gobbled it in one giant gulp.

"What was that?" asked Dr. George.

"What just happened?" asked his dad.

"What, no mayo?" asked the newborn.

Three

Most babies start walking right around their first birthday. But not Ruth Herman George ("Her Man" quickly became one word because his mother considered the capital letter M as unlucky as black cats, the number 13, or licking the rim of the ketchup bottle on a Tuesday). Ruth Herman George walked at two months old. He ran at three months old. And he slid headfirst into his bed at four months old.

What did he do at five months old? Well, no one knows how his family's house suddenly got a brand-new roof one morning, but the kid had gotten up very early that day, his parents were still sleeping, and the neighbors did hear a very young voice saying, "Ruth make roof, Ruth make roof, Ruth make roof," over and over and over again.

On the boy's first birthday, just as his mother and dad were singing, "Happy birthday dear Ruth Herman Georrrrge...," there was a sharp knock at the front door. But no one heard it, and the man who was knocking just walked away.

The parents watched in delight as their son blew out the candle and ate his entire cake. They were even more delighted as he burped a cute little burp, looked up at them and said, "Again…no mayo?"

Exactly 312 days later, Ruth Herman George was walking in the park with his grandmother. They walked past a baseball field, and the little boy took his grandmother's hand and said, "Grandmother, someday I will hit majestic home runs on a field just like this one."

His grandmother, somewhat deaf, thought he had said, "I'd like to climb into a tank of piranha and play chess with them at the aquarium." She laughed and laughed at the silliness of his comment—after all, the boy should have known that the aquarium was closed on Thursdays!

Just as they were leaving the park, a mighty home-run ball whizzed over the ball field fence. It was still climbing and heading right toward Ruth's grandmother! Without even thinking, the boy grabbed her cane and swatted the ball back toward the field. It flew over all the outfielders and infielders, and right into the catcher's glove! The ball got there just as the batter finished his jog around the bases, and the catcher tagged him out.

No one had ever seen anything like that before. Because no one had ever seen a slugger like almost-two-year-old Ruth Herman George.

As the boy trotted around imaginary bases, both teams' managers ran to the outfield fence and helped Ruth's grandmother back to her feet (without her cane, she'd just gone thud). Then they each offered contracts for the boy to join their teams.

"$100 a game, guaranteed!" said the first.

"$200 a game and a shiny new bicycle!" said the second.

Grandmother stood and thought about it. Then she said what was uppermost in her mind: "I really could use a piece of dental floss."

Ruth Herman George and his grandmother walked home in silence that day. But there was no denying the very real pride the boy felt inside. And there was also no denying the very real broccoli the grandmother felt inside her upper left wisdom tooth, made all the worse by the fact that she hadn't eaten broccoli for well over 17 years.

Four

Never mind that he was bigger than any teacher in the school. Never mind that he didn't fit into any of the classroom chairs, or that the art table flew across the room when he put his knees under it. And never mind that crayons exploded as soon as he grasped them.

Ruth Herman George was five years old, and it was time for him to attend kindergarten at Abner Tripleday Elementary School.

Mrs. Inzero, the smiling teacher, looked at the thirty-seven kids in the brightly colored classroom and said, "Okay boys and girls, let's line up! Say who you are by last name first, first name last."

"Where does the middle name go?" asked the biggest boy in the class.

"In the middle, of course," Mrs. Inzero informed him. "Where else *would it go*?"

"Well, since you're moving around the first and last names, I thought maybe the middle name was going somewhere else, too," the boy offered.

"I'm confused," said little Johnson Baines Lyndon."

"Me, too," said Harris Patrick Neil (who later became very, very famous for something that has nothing to do with this story).

Confusion reigned, and as it did, there was a sharp knock at the classroom door. But no one heard it, and the man who was knocking just walked away.

The noise and chaos stopped when Sheri Adams finally swooped to the front of the line and said, "Adams, Sheri."

"Very good," said Mrs. Inzero.

Marcy Aardvark jumped in front of Sue and said, "Aardvark, Marcy."

"That's fine," said Mrs. Inzero.

"Not with me, it's not," said Adams, Sheri. "I wanted to be first."

Other students quickly announced their last names/first names and took their places. Then the big boy in the class said, "George, Herman Ruth."

"No, George, last name first," said Mrs. Inzero.

"That *is* my last name," the boy answered.

"Now George..." she exclaimed.

"No, my name is Ruth," he said.

"Ruth Herman George?" she asked.

"Yes, Ruth Herman George."

"I've asked you to say last name first, first name last," the teacher said.

"I did. And middle name in the middle."

The teacher raised her voice.

"Young man, I'm asking you to say your name backward, and you keep doing it backward."

"Which is good, right?" he asked hopefully.

"No! Say, 'Ruth, Herman George,' then go stand with the Rs, Master George Herman Ruth," Mrs. Inzero firmly replied.

The boy did what the teacher said, taking his place between Roberts, Debbie and Ryan, James.

To him, the whole thing seemed Ridiculous, Totally. But he went along with it and decided three things that very morning:

1. Someday he'd be known by a really wonderful nickname. Or several.
2. Someday he'd be known by a number.
3. Someday he'd remember to wear pants to school.

Five

George Herman Ruth, as he came to be known, was a terrific school athlete. Between kindergarten and fourth grade, he broke more than fourteen school records and more than twenty-seven school windows (actually, he broke fifteen school records and twenty-eight school windows, which probably would have been easier to let you know in the first place).

At recess, he singlehandedly beat the rest of the class in volleyball, dodgeball, kickball, wall ball, paddleball, handball, and Georgeball (a game he invented and always won because he wouldn't teach anyone else how to play).

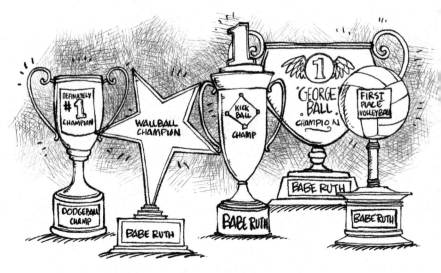

But it was in baseball that he really stood out.

He was awarded Athlete of the Day, Athlete of the Week, Athlete of the Year, Athlete of the Decade, and Athlete of the Century.

Everyone wanted to play like him. Everyone wanted to be like him. And everyone wanted to be his friend (Ruby Schwartz so desperately wanted to stand near him in line, she legally changed her name to Schwartz Ruby).

Oh sure, there were some problems in school, such as the day George Herman Ruth was almost blinded in a punctuation accident, or the time he jumped on the playground seesaw and sent Phil Waldman to the hospital (literally, he plopped on it with such force that Phil flew across the street and into a fifth-floor hospital room. Fortunately, Phil landed on a well-cushioned hospital bed and was uninjured. Unfortunately, though, it was well cushioned with Mrs. Inzero's husband, who was lying on it at the time and suffered a collapsed lung, a collapsed rib cage, and a collapsed bed).

But perhaps the most memorable day in George Herman Ruth's school career happened at precisely 12:46:08 p.m. on Tuesday, December 17th—though no one wrote down which year.

That's the exact moment when George Herman Ruth looked down into his daily quart of tapioca pudding and saw that the raisins on top miraculously spelled out BABEK.

The boy couldn't believe it! He looked down and said the word: BABEK. What a wonderful nickname for a great and mighty slugger! BABEK!

He grabbed the megaphone he always kept nearby and announced to the lunchroom crowd, "Now stepping up to bat...the great and mighty slugger, BABEK GEORGE HERMAN RUTH!"

Before anyone could respond, he noticed that the last letter in BABEK wasn't raisins, but rather a cluster of ants that traveled in the form of the letter K. As they scampered off, the boy made the following correction...

"Correction, now stepping up to bat...the great and mighty slugger, BABE GEORGE HERMAN RUTH!"

"That's too long a name," someone shouted from lunch table Nine.

"Correction, now stepping up to bat...the great and mighty slugger, BABE GEORGE HERMAN!"

"Try it another way," someone shouted from lunch table Four.

"Correction, now stepping up to bat...the great and mighty slugger, BABE HERMAN RUTH!"

"Hey, my bag of chips is gone," someone shouted from lunch table Eleven. *"And shorten that name!"*

"Correction, now stepping up to bat...the great and mighty slugger, BABE RUTH!"

"Yaaay," everyone cheered.

The great and mighty slugger had found his nickname. And even better, he had found the bag of chips the kid at lunch table Eleven was missing.

Babe Ruth decided that the chips—and his new nickname—were equally delicious (though the chips were crunchy, and the nickname wasn't).

Six

Babe Ruth sailed through middle school, which made his parents proud, but angered his principal, since they didn't allow boats in the hallways. So after that, he walked.

Speaking of walking, that's something Babe did a lot of while playing baseball for the Abner Tripleday Middle School team.

Frankly, other teams didn't want to face his mighty swing. So they intentionally walked him almost every time up. Sometimes opposing hurlers would pitch from second base, 'cause Babe hit the ball back with such force, it'd smack them in the face and get permanently lodged in their noses.

Just ask Dave Stepman, who had the misfortune of catching a ball in his left nostril.

The nostril bled for twenty-seven days, but Dave's doctor decided he didn't need stitches because, after all, there were stitches on the ball.

Eventually, no one wanted to pitch to Babe. So, he offered to pitch to himself. That's right, he stood on the mound and threw the ball, then raced to home plate, picked up a bat, and swung his mighty swing. The good news is he smacked twenty-five home runs against himself in exactly twenty-five swings. The bad news, of course, was that his earned run average as a pitcher was...infinity.

Still, there was something that made his coach think Babe could be a pretty excellent pitcher. The coach walked up to his favorite player one afternoon and said, "Babe, there's something that makes me think you could be a pretty excellent pitcher."

Babe was quite flattered, and told his coach that as soon as he was done peeing, he'd be thrilled to talk about it with him. And that's just what happened.

Moments later, Babe and the coach shared an official handshake to celebrate the idea that Babe would be the starting pitcher at every game the rest of the season.

Babe was very, very happy.

So was the coach, though he did wish Babe had washed his hand before the official handshake.

Seven

Amazingly, Babe Ruth completed high school in eleven minutes, without taking a single class. At the graduation party, which was held with all the participants on horseback, everyone was talking about their career goals.

The Ringling Brothers and their friends, Barnum and Bailey, announced they were going to be plumbers.

Charlie Lindbergh declared he wanted to be a bus driver.

And Alice Arnold told everyone she was going to invent the stain.

Babe didn't say a word during the whole conversation.

Later that day, back at home, Babe's mother said to him, "So, Mr. Mighty Swing, how are you going to make a living now?"

Babe thought about it.

"Yes, Mr. Mighty Swing, how are you going to make a living now?" his father echoed.

Babe thought about it some more.

The whole room was silent again until Babe's grandmother started hopping up and down, shrieking...

"I've got it! I've got it! I've got it, I've got it, I've got it!"

"Wow, Grandmother, you know how I'm going to make a living?" Babe asked hopefully.

"Naw! Remember that broccoli that's been stuck in my teeth? I've got it!"

It was a sad, seemingly hopeless situation. Then suddenly there was a sharp knock at the front door. But no one heard it, and the man who was knocking just walked away.

Later that afternoon, to help him decide what to do for a living, Babe made a list of all the things he was good at.

1. Hitting a baseball
2. Pitching a baseball
3. Catching a baseball
4. Throwing a baseball

Babe quickly realized that the items on his list had something in common: all four things he'd written down had the word "a" in them.

Babe studied the list some more. And he finally, finally, finally, (finally) realized that they all involved baseball! He'd be a baseball player!

Then suddenly there was a sharp knock at the front door. Babe opened the door and saw a man in a gray suit. And by the way, it was not the same man who'd knocked on doors so many times before.

"Nice suit," Babe said. "Come in and sit

down anywhere but on the blue chair, 'cause that's where my grandmother is sitting right now."

The man smiled, entered, and explained that he was a scout from a major league baseball team that wanted Babe to play for them! Real baseball. For real money!

Babe was thrilled.

Babe's mother was thrilled.

Babe's father was thrilled.

Babe's grandmother was thrilled.

And when Babe signed his name on the sixty-three-page contract (written entirely

in Swahili) and officially shook the scout's hand, the scout was thrilled, too.

Though he did wish Babe had washed his hand before the official handshake.

Eight

Ninety-nine percent of all major leaguers start their baseball careers in the minor leagues. But not Babe. He was asked to join the Cubs big league club for spring training, and that's what he did.

Babe arrived wearing the team uniform his grandmother had knitted for him. She'd also made him a pair of red socks, which he proudly wore.

The Cubs manager was so impressed with Babe's red socks that he immediately asked Babe's grandmother to knit a pair for everyone on the team—and he was inspired to change the name of the team to honor her handiwork.

From that moment on, the team became known as the Boston Red Knitted Itchy Foot Coverings.

Fueled by very large pre- and post-game meals, Babe pitched brilliantly and slugged tremendous home runs throughout spring training, and by opening day, his fame, his legend, and his waistline were enormous.

The newspaper headlines said it all:

Opening day: How Many Will Babe Hit?

Will Babe Pitch a Perfect Game on Day One?

If You're Coming to the Game on Opening Day, Bring Your Own Food. Babe Ate Everything They Had at the Stadium

When Babe saw his name written on the opening day lineup card, he cried. Yes, the boy born as Ruth Herman George was quite moved by all that had happened to him; he'd gotten a nickname that everyone knew, he had a number on his back, he'd made the major leagues, and in a moment, he was about to actually play on the very same big-league field.

He dried his tears with the lineup card and then ate it—both for good luck and for the healthful fiber it contained. That's something he would do at every major league game in which he played.

When the ump yelled, "Play ball," Babe wound up and threw such a sweeping curve that the batter actually swung at it and missed three times.

"Yer out!" yelled the ump.

The crowd of 55,001 cheered Babe's one-pitch strikeout. They cheered again when he did the same thing to the next batter. And they cheered again when he did the same thing to the next batter after that.

Three pitches. Three strikeouts. A baseball record!

The ump motioned for Babe and his team to leave the field. But Babe asked for more batters to come up and face him, telling the ump, "Listen, I'm here...I might as well strike everyone out in the second, third, and fourth innings, too!"

And that's just what happened.

Babe pitched a three-hit shutout that day. He also hit two home runs and knocked in seven. What a day! What a ballplayer!

After the game, Babe signed more than 250 autographs outside the team clubhouse, including one to, of all people, Alice Arnold.

He winked and smiled at Alice and signed her scorecard:

Hi Alice, don't give up trying to invent the stain. I know you can do it! Your fiend, Babe Alice really appreciated the kind message from her high school friend, and later added an "r" so it said, "Your friend" instead of "Your fiend." But that added "r" never fooled anyone, since Babe had signed in red ink, and she wrote in the extra letter in green.

Nine

With Babe striking out batters and hitting homers at a record pace, the team won championship after championship after championship. One year they even won the National Hockey League trophy—the Stanley Cup—which was awarded to Babe and his teammates by none other than Mr. Cup himself.

But Babe wasn't destined to play ball in those itchy, red socks forever. On a slightly cloudy November day, with the threat of showers hanging over the whole town (though it didn't actually rain), and temperatures in the mid-40s, and the wind chill somewhere

in the 30s, with winds blowing from the
north-northeast at 15-20 miles per hour and
quite a bit of traffic due to construction in
many parts of the city, Babe was sold to
another team for a lot, lot, lot of money.

The owner called Babe and told him he'd
been sold to a rival ballclub. Their conversation is one the owner will never forget, though
it's been about 85 years since his death.

Owner: "Babe, you don't play for us any-
more."

Babe: "Okay."

When the next season started, Babe
showed up and was immediately given a
white uniform with horizontal red pin-

stripes. He put it on and immediately laid down to take a nap.

The owner of his new team walked by and saw his very large, very expensive player in his new uniform. And...seeing the then-vertical pinstripes on the sleeping Babe gave the owner an idea—he immediately had the team tailor switch all the uniforms to vertical pinstripes.

When Babe woke up, everyone around him was wearing vertical pinstripes, and his were horizontal. Babe looked at the shortstop. He looked at the second basemen. He looked at the outfielders and the catcher. They were all in vertical pinstripes. His were clearly very, very different.

But Babe never noticed.

Babe also never noticed that the number on his uniform back had changed. After all, it's very, very hard to see your own back. On his previous team, he'd worn number 47. But after spending a lot, lot, lot of money to purchase Babe's contract, his new team didn't have much left for uniform numbers. So they just had the tailor write a large number 3— in beef gravy—on the back of Babe's uniform. Again, Babe never noticed. But he sure liked the smell and eventually asked for his uniform number to be written (again, in gravy) on his pants, his shoes, and his hat.

Babe's new manager loved how Babe pitched. But even more, he loved how he hit. And since pitchers don't usually play more than every fourth or fifth day, the coach walked up to his favorite player one afternoon and said, "Babe, you're an excellent pitcher, and I have an idea I'd like to discuss with you."

Babe was quite flattered and told his coach that as soon as he was done peeing, he'd be thrilled to talk about it with him. And that's just what happened.

Moments later, Babe and the manager shared an official handshake to celebrate the idea that Babe would become a starting outfielder—and would be able to play in every game all season.

Babe was very, very happy.

So was the manager, though he did wish Babe had washed his hand before the official handshake.

Ten

"The Big Guy in the Horizontal Pinstripes Even Though the Rest of the Team is Wearing Vertical Pinstripes" was Babe's nickname during his playing days.

Needless to say, he wasn't crazy about that.

And Babe continued to smash the ball as an outfielder, hitting more, out-homering every other ballplayer in the league. In fact, he hit more homers than *all the other play-ers combined*—a feat so impressive that it just had to be typed in italics.

Off the field, Babe was the life of the party, always out in fancy restaurants, seeing fancy shows, and petting fancy animals in fancy zoos. But Babe was, well, often lonely.

That all changed the day his mother called and told him she'd met a lovely young girl and thought marriage was a wonderful idea. Babe told her that she was being silly, since his mother was already married—to his father. But once Babe's mother said she thought *he* should meet and marry this girl, Babe understood. He agreed, saying, "I agree, Mother."

And the very day they met, Babe proposed, bought a house, and later put a diamond baseball glove on her hand so they could become man and wife. Incredibly, that young lady was the little girl whose iPhone he'd broken years before. But though they stayed married for the rest of his life, neither of them ever realized the connection.

After getting married, Babe became very interested in helping the less fortunate. He often threw large, mostly uneaten turkey legs out of his car window to feed those in need, a gesture that most of the recipients greatly appreciated—unless he whacked them in the head, of course.

He also spent a great deal of time visit-

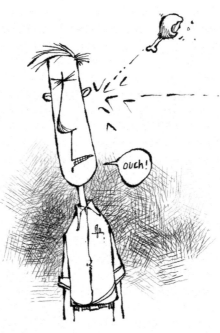

ing children's hospitals, cheering little tykes who were big baseball fans. Often he'd chat with the kids, signing autographs, giving batting tips, and inviting them to "get better and c'mon out to see me play!"

Often if Babe had extra time during a hospital visit, he'd put on a mask and perform a surgery or two, whether the patients needed them or not. And because he was a generous guy, he never charged for these operations—and even paid out of his own pocket for doctors to replace the parts that Babe had removed for fun.

A reporter once asked Babe, "Isn't it hard to perform surgery without a lick of medical training?"

And Babe replied, "Hitting a fast ball five hundred feet is hard. Yanking out an appendix is a piece of cake!"

Then, for good measure, he removed the reporter's appendix and had a piece of cake.

Eleven

By the time Babe Ruth ended his playing career, he owned pretty much every record a slugger could achieve.

Most home runs in a game.

Most home runs in a season.

Most lifetime home runs.

Most RBIs in a game.

Most RBIs in a season.

Most lifetime RBIs.

Most burgers eaten while on third base.

And most autographs signed on pretzels.

For Babe's last game, the league allowed him to be the only batter for his team—he played right field and batted first, second, third, fourth, fifth, sixth, seventh, eighth, and ninth.

Babe homered each and every time up, which was very fortunate, 'cause it would have been a big problem if he'd singled and then had to get up to bat to try to drive himself in.

Moments after the final out was made in Babe's final game, the Commissioner of Baseball stepped onto the field and made an extremely moving speech about Babe and his contributions to the game of baseball:

"Babe, you have hit so many home runs and touched so many lives with your kindness, your spirit, and your generosity, that everyone in baseball, everyone who watches baseball, and anyone who's ever seen a baseball owe you a debt of gratitude. You are a great, great hitter and a great, great man."

Unfortunately, Babe was in the clubhouse eating a bat-sized salami that was signed by his entire team—and didn't hear a word of the speech.

After retiring from the game he loved, Babe Ruth became a symphony conductor, a Latin teacher, a shoe salesman, and a chocolate dipper in a candy factory. He often stopped by ball fields and gave kids free advice on how to be mighty sluggers, though no one could come close to what he'd achieved.

Babe's records lasted many years longer than Babe himself did.

He died on March 5th in a year too sad to mention. His wife was by his side, as was Alice Arnold, who'd stopped by to show Babe that she had indeed finally invented the stain.

Babe's last words were truly memorable and inspiring. Just before he closed his eyes for the last time, Babe said, "I never got the mayo."

Upon hearing of his death, the Commissioner of Baseball made an extremely moving speech about Babe and his contributions to the game of baseball:

"Babe hit so many home runs and touched so many lives with his kindness, his spirit, and his generosity, everyone in baseball, everyone who watches baseball, and anyone who's ever seen a baseball owe him a debt of gratitude. He was a great, great hitter and a great, great man."

Once again, of course, Babe didn't hear him.

★ ★ ★ ★ ★ ★ ★ ★

Okay, now that you've read *The Lieography of Babe Ruth*, you're probably wondering about the real-life story of the great, great ballplayer.

Well, you're in luck; here are some factual facts about the man. You can believe everything you're about to read, and it'd be great if you check out even more information about him.

George Herman Ruth Jr. was born in Baltimore, Maryland, on February 6, 1895. Because he was a bit of a troublemaker as a young boy, his parents sent him to live at St. Mary's Industrial School for Boys. It was there that he developed a great love of baseball.

Brother Matthias, one of the Catholic monks at the school, worked with George to improve the young man's pitching, batting, and fielding skills. Eventually, George became so good that he attracted the attention of Jack Dunn, the owner of the Baltimore Orioles.

Mr. Dunn signed 19-year-old George to a contract in 1914, and the Orioles players referred to George as "Jack's newest babe." The nickname stuck.

Soon after, newly named Babe was sold to the Boston Red Sox.

Interestingly, although Babe would set records as a powerful slugger, he started his career as a pitcher. And while he had several successful seasons on the mound, he was such a mighty hitter that the team decided they needed him in the lineup every day. Therefore, in 1918, he began playing the outfield.

A year later, Babe was sold to the New York Yankees; that's where the slugger *really* started mashing the ball. In 1920, for example, Babe hit 54 home runs (no one else in the league hit more than 19 that year!). How did Babe top himself in 1921? By pounding 59 homers and collecting 171 runs batted in.

Babe's legend grew and grew; in 1923, when the Yankees moved to a new ballpark, it was known as "The House That Ruth Built."

The story is often told that in a 1932 game against the Cubs, Babe pointed to center field. Then, he hit the very next pitch over the fence—exactly where he had pointed. Simply incredible!

Beyond being called Babe, Mr. Ruth had quite a few other nicknames, including "The Great Bambino," "The Big Bam," and "The Sultan of Swat." Over his 22 seasons as a Major Leaguer, Babe hit 714 regular-season home runs (he also won 94 games as a pitcher). Quite simply, he stood alone as a ballplayer; no other athlete came close to matching his accomplishments on the field. Babe's mighty blasts were dubbed "Ruthian"—and that's a term that's still used today to describe a colossal sports achievement.

In many ways, Babe achieved a greater level of success and popularity than any other public figure of his time. Everyone wanted to follow his daily exploits. Maybe that's why *The New York Times* called him a national curiosity.

Even after his playing days were done, Babe Ruth was a larger-than-life figure; he performed on radio shows and in movies (he played himself in *Pride of the Yankees,* a biographical movie about his teammate Lou Gehrig). Babe attracted a crowd everywhere he went; he was a big man, with a big appetite for life, a big personality, and a big heart (he often visited sick kids in the hospital).

Babe Ruth passed away in 1948. And while some of his baseball records have since been broken, Babe stands alone, both as an athlete and a highly regarded figure. Even today, more than eighty-five years after he retired from baseball, most people consider Babe Ruth to be the greatest baseball player who's ever lived.

Man, could that guy hit!

Author's Bio

Alan Katz has written more than 40 highly acclaimed children's books, including *Take Me Out of the Bathtub and Other Silly Dilly Songs, The Day the Mustache Took Over, OOPS!, Don't Say That Word!, Really Stupid Stories for Really Smart Kids*, and two *Awesome Achievers* titles. Alan has received many state awards for children's literature, and he frequently speaks at literacy conferences and schools around the country.

Alan is also a six-time Emmy-nominated writer for series including *The Rosie O'Donnell Show, Taz-Mania, Pinkalicious and Peterrific*, numerous Nickelodeon shows, and more. He hosted a long-running game show on SiriusXM's Kids Place Live channel, and he's also created comic books, trading cards, theme park shows, and hundreds of other special projects for kids and their parents.

Illustrator's Bio

Tracy Hill has been working as an illustrator since 1989, creating humorous and whimsical illustrations for clients in the advertising, editorial, and publishing fields. His true passion has been in illustrating children's books.

THANKS FOR READING
The Lieography of Babe Ruth.

Also pick up other Lieographies:

The Lieography of Thomas Edison

The Lieography of Amelia Earhart